These Texas hills are mine
nd where a trail grows dim
I mark its course again
ith simple verse and hymn.

That Spotted Sow
and Other Texas
Hill Country Ballads

Foreword

People cherish Carlos Ashley's warm-hearted verse. "The man writes in pictures," Cowboy Kelly once told me. Cowboy Kelly, who died several years ago, was perhaps Texas' best primitive painter.

Kelly loved the title poem in this volume. In fact, after reading it he composed an oil painting of a spotted feral sow, and then Old Man Kelly caught the bus from his home in Blanket and went to Llano and presented the work of art to the poet. Few poets ever receive such spontaneous manifestations of appreciation.

To recite Carlos Ashley's endeavors suggests that he is really 2 or 3 men. He has been a hill country rancher all his life. He was an athlete at TCU and a high school coach for 3 years before going on to law school. He has had a distinguished legal career and was recently the chairman of a squad of lawyers writing a volume on the history and traditions of the Texas Bar.

He was a State Senator for 10 years and District Attorney of the Texas hill country for 18. He is a 3rd generation hill country rancher, and for many years he has raised and raced thoroughbred horses in that ideal horse country. His kudos are too many to mention, but it should be recited that he is a former Poet Laureate of Texas, which was only fair since he writes the sort of verse that probably appeals to the most in Texas.

I somehow wandered into a sort of convention of Texas poets in Dallas about a decade ago and heard Carlos recite some of his poems, verse in praise of creatures in the range from the town scavenger in San Saba, Texas, to the former Vice President of the United States, Cactus Jack Garner.

My favorite Carlos Ashley poem is called "Bob Sears' Chili Joint." This is an ode in nostalgic remembrance of a little chili parlor in Carlos' home town, San Saba.

For one thing he admitted in the opening lines:

"There's a smell about good chili
That no poet can portray . . . . .
And of all exotic odors
That the wings-of-time anoint,
There's none can match description
With Bob Sears' chili joint . . . . . "

Carlos mentioned some of the famous eating places in New York City and New Orleans where he'd dined, and then he wound up his classic chili poem with these lines:

"Yet no chef has ever challenged
The high gastronomic point
That was mine in early childhood
In Bob Sears' Chili Joint."

I've nominated Carlos Ashley for poet laureate of the Chili Appreciation Society International. And the barbers of Texas should make Carlos their poet laureate for his beautiful tribute in verse to the town tonsorial artist, called "Jim Watkins' Barber Shop."

This book is valuable, too, because it is illustrated by pen-and-ink sketches of the hill country and its people and its creatures, such as quarter horses and coyotes, by one of the memorable of western artists, the late Harold D. Bugbee of Clarendon, Texas.

FRANK TOLBERT
Dallas Morning News Daily Columnist

Contents

THAT SPOTTED SOW *(The Ballad of Cedar Mountain)*	9
BOB SEARS' CHILI JOINT	14
WILD CATTLE	15
JIM WATKINS' BARBER SHOP	16
EPILOGUE	17
THE WIDDER	18
OLE EDGAR MARTIN	21
OH, WHERE IS THAT RIVER?	23
TRUE LIVIN	25
TEXAN'S CODE	26
SO-LONG	27
SCIENCE — ROMANCE	28
SOUTH OF THE CAP ROCK	29
FOR POLITICIANS	30
AUNT CORDIE	31
LUCK	34
THE DESTINY STAKES	35
LOVE AND A SONG	36
THE CEDAR-WHACK	37
SAID THE HOOT OWL TO THE HEN HAWK	38
BOWIE'S BONES	39
THE KING OF THE COUNTY FAIR	41
THE SUBSTITUTE	43
DUTY	44
A SERMON	45
OLD BLUE	47
VALUES	49
BLACKSNAKE BILL	50
THE BIG CONVENTION	53
SERVICE	55
I BUILT MY HOUSE UPON A HILL	55
AMBITION	56
THE SHERIFF'S WIDOW	57
THE OLD NIGHTWATCHMAN	59
HARD TIMES	60
PETE WOOD'ARD	61
YOUR EYES ARE BROWN	62
NYLON AVENUE	63

WHAT IS A FLOWER?	64
THE OLD TOWN CLOCK	65
THE TICKET	66
HUMAN NATURE	66
BONNIE BIRD (1890–1917)	67
ABE GALLOWAY	69
CACTUS JACK	70
WHEN THE WORLD GETS OUT OF FOCUS	72

That Spotted Sow
or The Ballad of Cedar Mountain

Did you ever hear the story
  Of that famous hog of mine?
She's a razorback and spotted
  Black and white from hoof to spine;

With a snout made outa granite,
  She can root just like a plow;
And the fence aint been invented
  That can turn that spotted sow.

Born and bred on Cedar Mountain,
  She is wilder than a deer;
And she's known by reputation
  To the ranch hands far and near.

Though a sow of mine had raised 'er,
  On that mountain she was free;
And I always kinda doubted
  That she really b'longed to me.

She didn't claim no owner —
  Save the God who put 'er there —
And for mortal man's relations
  She just simply didn't care.

She preferred the solemn silence
    Of her Cedar Mountain home,
And most of all she wanted us
    To let 'er plum alone.

Ever Fall I'd try to mark 'er,
    But she'd get away agin;
And I reckon that my cussin,
    Though artistic, was a sin.

Well, I sold my brand in '30 —
    Moved out ever hog and cow;
Rounded-up . . . yeah . . . all but one head,
    All but that blamed spotted sow.

So we organized against 'er—
    Got the best of dogs and men;
But we never got good started
    Puttin that hog in a pen.

Now we really went a-huntin
    When we tried to catch Ole Spot;
We left the ranch at daylight
    And her trail was always hot.

She might be pickin acorns
    On the banks of Sandy Creek,
Or in somebody's turnips
    Cultivatin, so to speak.

But let the foot of dog or man
    Disturb the mornin dew,
And you might as well a phoned 'er,
    'Cause, somehow, she always knew.

She'd light out for Cedar Mountain,
    Where the land and sky divide—
There aint no spot on earth nowhere
    A better place to hide.

We'd hear the pack a-bayin
    Up the mountain loud and clear,
But before we rode up to 'em
    That ole sow would disappear.

Or she'd rally 'gainst a boulder,
    Bristlin like a porcupine,
Till a dog forgot his caution—
    Then she'd cut him into twine.

Killin dogs was just a pastime
    To that hog; I'm tellin you,
With them long, curved, knife-like tushes
    She could slice a houn in two.

She could whip most any critter
    On four legs I ever saw,
And she had a perfect record
    'Cause she never fought a draw.

Now the more I tried to catch 'er,
   And the more I give it thought,
I begin to get the notion
   She's opposed to bein caught.

I couldn't help admire that sow,
   When all was done and said;
For, to tell the truth about 'er,
   She was really thoroughbred.

She had character and courage
   And the heart to do the right;
And when it come to fightin,
   Now she shore as hell could fight.

Well, the Fall froze into Winter,
   And the Winter thawed to Spring.
April watered hill and valley;
   Maytime painted ever'thing.

Late one evenin just at sundown
   I was ridin home right slow,
   When I passed a lonesome waterhole
   And saw . . . . . . it was a show.

Ole Spot was trailin down the hill
   And right behind her trotted
Ten baby pigs not ten days old,
   And ever one was spotted.

I stopped and stared; she studied me;
   My eyes filled like a fountain;
And there I gave Ole Spot a deed—
   A deed to Cedar Mountain.

Now I was taught that folks who try,
   You oughta help and praise 'em;
So, "Boys," I sez, "Ole Spot's got pigs,
   And, damn shore gonna raise 'em."

She's still on Cedar Mountain,
   Though I seldom see 'er now;
You can bet that's one dominion
   Where the Queen's a spotted sow.

Bob Sears' Chili Joint

There's a smell about good chili
That no poet can portray;
   It wafts a rare aroma
Where the gentle breezes play;
   And of all exotic ordors
That the wings-of-time anoint,
   There's none can match description
With Bob Sears' Chili Joint.

   Now it wasn't much to look at,
Just a hole there in the wall,
   No sign above the entrance
And no fancy front atall.
   A stranger couldn't find it
'Less the wind was blowin right;
   Then he couldn't hardly miss it,
Even on the darkest night.

   A dime would buy a bowl full
Of that wondrous bill-of-fare;
A quarter got a milk shake
And another bowl to spare.
   It wasn't always fresh and clean
By sanitations's letter,
   But somehow it improved with age
And day by day got better.

   I've eaten Antoine's Crepe Suzettes,
A joy beyond compare;

I've dined at old Delmonicos',
Where famed gourmets repair;
But no Chef has ever challenged
The high gastronomic point
That was mine in early childhood
In Bob Sears' Chili Joint.

Wild Cattle

The Years stampede-by like a herd of wild cattle;
A stompin and beller'n they surge through the land;
If you aint purty sharp you'll get run plum over,
And the feller that heads 'em is shore nuf a hand.

The years rumble-on through the rocks and the cedars,
They keep gettin wilder, it seems like to me;
They tear down the fences and make such a racket
And stir up the dust til you cant hardly see.

A feller needs help workin that kind of cattle:
A set of good pens and a cow horse to ride,
True friends and real neighbors, and knowin for certain
That him and the Big Boss are on the same side.

Jim Watkins' Barber Shop

There are many institutions
That deserve our public praise;
   They've enriched the lives of millions
In as many different ways;
   You can list them by the dozen,
But there's one I rate the top,
   For I got my education
In Jim Watkins' Barber Shop.

   There the school kids used to gather
'Til the glow of setting sun
   Dragged our lagging footsteps homeward,
Late to get the night-work done.
   There the Field-of-Life was fertile,
Watered with a zest and joy
   That are always boon companions
Of a wide-eyed country boy.

   Ah, the hopes we fondly kindled
In that richly perfumed air;
   Oh, how many dreams of conquest
Were inspired and nurtured there.
   We enshrined our childhood heroes
In our hearts and on the walls,
   And no pictures are their equals
In the world's museum halls.

   There the great Manassa Mauler
Won his crown that hot July;

There in later years he lost it
As we mourned with tear-dimned eye.
 Ruth and Hornsby, Cobb and Sisler,
Gotch and Lewis—ah-h Pet Brown,
 King of Middleweights from Texas,
Pal of every kid in town.

 Passing years stilled many voices
Of my friends of boyhood days,
 But I yearn and hunger for them
In a hundred different ways;
 So I think I'll go a-visiting
And I don't intend to stop
 'Til I'm sitting in the shine-chair
Of Jim Watkins' Barber Shop.

Epilogue

Ambition feeds a thousand fires
Whose ashes leave no ember;
I pray to pen a rustic rhyme
That someone will remember.

The Widder

It gits kinda lonesome out on the divide
    With never a woman aroun,
So about twice a year I saddle Ole Bell
    And ride down the canyon to town.

I been sorter courtin a widder down there,
    Though I aint never out and proposed;
We been a-maneuver'n and sparrin aroun,
    And we had the deal just about closed.

Course a man must be cautious where women's
        concerned—
    It's a trail over mighty thin ice—
I been livin single for fifty-two year
    While the widder, she's been married twice.

These females is mighty peculiar at times
    And awful deceitful to figger;
The things that seem little before you git hitched
    Next mornin may look a heap bigger.

So I been debatin this matter since Fall,
    Which, in fact, was the last time I seen 'er;
But the sap started risin right early this Spring,
    And the grass and the trees all looked greener

Than I could remember since I was a kid,
    And the bluebonnets bigger and bluer;

And the reasons for living out here all alone
   Seemed to fade and grow fewer and fewer.

   The trail down the canyon seemed smoother that day,
   And the mockin'birds sang a lot louder;
It mighta been me or the moon bein full,
   Or the smell of her perfume and powder.

It could be her cookin that lulled me to sleep—
   Them was wonderful biscuits and pies—
Or her tender, melodious voice as she sang
   With a heavenly light in her eyes.

Whatever it was, it shore done the job;
   I was just gittin ready to ast 'er,
When all of a sudden the front doorbell rang
   And who do you reckon? ——— the pastor.

Maybe I'm too suspicious of womenfolk's ways,
   But I shore know a church by its steeple;
And I know ever preacher on top side of earth
   Is dead set on marryin people.

The sight of that feller give me a cold chill;
   My pulse took to jumpin and poundin.
Him "sistern" and "brothern" all over the place—
   I felt for a fact like I's drowndin.

My heart turned a cat when that parson walked in;
   The sweat started wiltin my collar.
That room was a furnace plum bakin my brain,
   And I knowed I was goin to holler.

I was just gittin set for one desperate lunge
   For my hat 'cross the room on the dresser,
When the voice of an angel came out of the night:
   Ole Bell was a-nicker'n, God bless 'er.

I lied to that widder: my horse wasn't fed—
   Ah-h-h, the air was a tonic outside—
I rode all that night, and I didn't slow down
   Till I got back out on the divide.

I reckon I'll stay here the rest of my days;
   I aint goin back into town;
I'll take mine a-batchin and pamper'n Ole Bell—
   We don't need no woman aroun.

Ole Edgar Martin

I seen Ole Edgar Martin a-ridin by jus now;
   He's goin up to Walker's to get that bald-faced cow.
Funny feller—Edgar—sorter quiet and queer—
   Why, he's been ridin by that way for nearly twenty year.

I knowed 'im when he's jest a kid a-livin at his aunt's—
   A-wearin long-tailed hickry shirts 'thout no boots ner pants;
Sorter shied from other kids—his folks wuz all that way—
   A-grazin off from all the herd jus like a maverick stray.

He growed up in these post oak hills, a-huntin fox and coon—
   Hell, I can hear his ole houn now a-bayin to the moon
While boy and dog come down this flat—there warn't
     much town here then—
   Yeh, Edgar had a world o range to run them varmints in.

But my, this town has changed a sight—it aint the
     same a-tall;
   They've put in City Water Works and built a City Hall
And Edgar's changed a heap hisself—he aint quite
     understood
   That all the things he's honin for are gone—and
     gone for good.

I reckon Edgar's sixty-five—a little feeble too—
   He never took to no one trade—aint much that he kin do.
So he jus rides aroun all day—a sorter "livin sigh"—
   A lost and homeless kinda look a-starin from his eye.

He starts at daylight for the hills, when herds is comin down,
    And helps the ranchers and the boys to punch their
        stuff through town.
He hangs aroun the pens all day to watch 'em load the cars—
    And nights—I've seen 'im on his porch jus lookin
        at the stars.

He's pickin up a little stuff for Bigg's Meat Market now—
    Like goin up to Walker's there to get that bald-faced cow.
I noticed when he passed jus now he didn't have no houn—
    So guess I'd better saddle-up and help 'im into town.

Oh, Where Is That River?

Oh, where is that river Pa told me about
    When I left for the Pecos this Spring?
I've rode and I've hunted nigh four hundred miles,
    And I don't b'lieve there is such a thing.

I'm dry as a powder house inside and out;
    My pony is draggin his tracks.
I aint sweat a drop in a week and a half,
    And this desert's so hot that it cracks.

Pa said it was hot down in Texas sometimes—
    But I was a venturesome squatter.
He didn't explain to me when I left home
    How a feller can live without water.

Them prairie dogs settin on top of their holes
    A-grinnin and twitchin their tails;
They know I'm a goner, just driftin around
    Like a ship on the sea with sails.

Them buzzards keep circlin around and around,
    Enjoyin my miserable groans.
They're lickin their chops till my saddle horse drops;
    Then they all will be pickin my bones.

Now I wouldn't demand a cool mountain brook
    In the heart of a deep forest glade,
If I could but see just one lonesome tree
    Where I could lie down in the shade.

If I ever get home and live to be wed,
    When I tell how I come close to dyin,
If I have me ten kids and they don't weep out loud,
    I'll whip the whole bunch for not cryin.

True Livin

I've had the opportunity
To contrast and compare
  A lot of towns and cities
And the folks a-livin there.

  Some people have the notion
That a city is the place
  Of a bountiful existence
For the entire human race.

  But as one who's dwelt among 'em
I can state, with due restraint,
  That there's no place like a city
Where the joys of livin aint.

  Why you hardly know your neighbors,
And your friends you love so true
  Might as well live in Alaska
For what good they're doin you.

  Yes, a big town was invented
Just to make friends grow apart—
  Cause ulcerated stomachs
And to chill the human heart.

  Sure it's fine to have ambition
And to strive to get ahead,
  But most likely you will wind up
With hard arteries instead.

Good folks are found in every clime,
But out where my folks live
   We'd never trade a cow hand
For a big executive.

   And experience has taught us
That true livin is an art
   That escapes most city people
And they really aint so smart.

   So I've weighed the facts and figgers
For their quality and worth
   And found these Texas Hills to be
The finest place on Earth.

Texan's Code

   If I berate or cuss your friend—
And whether wrong or right—
   Defend him on the instant
If you have to start a fight.

   And for a Texan's honor—
Whether man or horse or pup—
   Say something good about him—
If you have to make it up.

So-Long

I dream again of the days agone
   When I rode these hills with a six-gun on,
When I was young and the range was free
   And a rawhide saddle was home to me
          In the days agone.

I slept at night neath the starry sky,
   There lulled to rest by the screech owl's cry;
My brothers, the wolf and the plaintive loon,
   Watched while I slumbered beneath the moon
          And the starry sky.

But—ah-h—those times have passed away;
   I'm an old man now and my hair is gray;
My step is feeble—death knocks at the door—
   Soon I'll follow the riders who've gone before,
          Who have passed away.

As I sit each night in my cabin door
    With the moonlight streamin across the floor,
The howl of a wolf sounds dolefully,
    The voice of a brother callin me
        From my cabin door.

And my heart goes out to this comrade gray,
    For he, like me, has had his day;
He chants the end of the cowboy's song,
    And the hour has come for my last so-long
        To this comrade gray.

Science—Romance

We studied shells on the beach today
    And noted each shape and kind—
The fossils of starfish, subpectins and crabs,
Where the breakers crash on the jetties and slabs—
    And we named each shell we could find.

I lay in the sand on the beach today,
    With a shell of rainbow hue;
I listened to stories that sea shells tell,
And dreaming, I sailed in a magic spell—
    On the swell of the sweeping blue.

South of the Cap Rock

Oh, bury me South of the Cap Rock
Halfway to the Rio Grande,
Where the eagles sail
O'er the Spanish Trail
And the tall pecan trees stand.

Oh, my dreams are South of the Cap Rock,
Where the hills and rivers rise;
Where a sun-kissed peak
On the dimpled cheek
Of a Texas plateau lies.

Oh, it's springtime South of the Cap Rock,
And the bee-weeds blossom soon,
Where I used to ride
With my promised bride
Neath a lover's magic moon.

Now my heart lies South of the Cap Rock,
And there's where I want to die,
Near the Llano's brink
Where the cattle drink
And the nesting killdees cry.

Yes, bury me South of the Cap Rock
By my love on a granite hill,
And we will sleep
While the mountains keep
Their vigil, eternal, still.

For Politicians

   We need a little padlock
With a red light and a bell
   To hang upon the blabber-mouth
We use for "playin hell."

   The light would serve to warn us
Of the value of restraint—
   And that vocal diarrhea
Is our deadliest complaint.

   The little bell would interrupt
Fair oratory's flight—
   And, failing thus to staunch the flow,
Our good opponent might.

   The urge to be smart-alec
Is a hazardous pursuit—
   And our windy interjections
Bear as flatulent a fruit.

   So I think a little padlock
Might conserve a lot of breath
   Of word-eating politicians—
Who most always choke to death.

Aunt Cordie

You never did know Aunt Cordelia?
    They's a gap missin outa your life!
She was sure a remarkable woman—
    And I dreaded her worse'n my wife.

Her time was spent roundin up mavericks
    And brandin 'em out for the Lord;
Not many boys in this Hill Country
    Escaped from the wrath of her sword.

She contest-rule rode the Devil:
A-rakin in front and behind
She'd holler and come out a-fannin
    And kick 'im and beat 'im plum blind.

She worked at the job almost constant,
    And rode with a mighty sharp spur;
There aint airy houn dog a-livin
    That could smell any better'n her.

If I took a drink she could wind it.
    I'd heap rather be throwed in jail
Than to see Aunt Cordie a-comin—
    She made the worst sinners turn pale.

She caught us boys playin brush poker—
    The way she depicted our fate,
Our chances of crossin the Jordan
    Wasn't near good as fillin a straight.

So we promised we'd try to do better;
    We listened to Aunt Cordie pray
And wound up the meetin agreein
    We'd turn out for preachin next day.

We all edged in under the arbor
    And just kinda froze on the bench;
We stared straight ahead at the pulpit
    And didn't dare wiggle an inch.

Aunt Cordie was leadin the singin
   And playin the organ in style—
When she throwed back her head on
   "Old Canaan,"
   She could rattle the winders a mile.

The preacher was holdin revival—
   He knew more sad stories to tell
About the few people in Heav'm
   And the crowded condition in Hell.

The sinners seemed all time a-dyin—
   The flames were a-scorchin their hide;
The whole congregation was shoutin—
   My breast was a turmoil inside.

I lost count of time and location—
   That fire was a-cookin me brown.
Somebody was leadin me forward,
   And then we was both kneelin down.

Sure enough, Aunt Cordie had got me,
   And all of the other boys too;
We joined the church at that meetin
   Just like she had told us to do.

It's twenty years since that revival,
   But folks here remember it still,
When Aunt Cordie contested the Devil
   And rode him plum over the hill.

We buried her early last Summer,
    And all of the boys she had saved
She wanted to be her pallbearers
    And lay her away in her grave.

We fellers still meet and play poker
    And join in a drink now and then,
But drinkin a toast to Aunt Cordie
    Couldn't hardly be classed as a sin.

Luck

    A lucky boy am I to have
A wife so sweet and comely,
    While pore old Bill, he's got a wife
Who's mean as hell—and homely.

    Now for the majesty of law
I am an ardent rooter;
    But if I had a wife like Bill's—
I'll swear, I believe I'd shoot 'er.

    Yet if foul fate in fiendish jest
To such a hell should beckon—
    That kind of luck would guarantee
She'd shoot me first, I reckon.

The Destiny Stakes

Father Time's Racing Circuit,
Which each of us makes,
    Writes a final event
Called The Destiny Stakes.

    In this oldest of races
Tradition abounds,
    And its always renewed
At Pearly Gates Downs.

    Gabriel is the Starter,
Saint Peter the Judge,
    The weight that you carry
Is Lust, Greed and Grudge.

    You parade on your mount,
Named the Galloping Ghost,
    To the music of harps,
By the Heavenly Host.

    Its always called "fast"
That track in the sky,
    You get a fair start
To the Sweet Bye and Bye.

    You have to be ready
For the race any day,
    The Man lifts the latch
And you're off on your way.

    You never decline
When the post-trumpet sounds,
    For The Destiny Stakes
At Pearly Gates Downs.

Love and A Song

    A seed lay withered on the sand,
Deaf to creations' stern command,
    Until you sang; and lo, there glows
On desert's barren waste a rose.

    The sky, the plains, the hills, the sea,
And all of God's great symphony,
    Were meaningless, without design,
Until your song made them divine.

    What priceless gifts yours to bestow,
Beyond the depths of man to know;
    Yet measureless to me belong
Your treasures all; love and a song.

The Cedar-Whack

The North wind howls like a timber wolf
    As it snaps at the flappin door
On the duckin shack of the cedar-whack
    And his kids on the damp dirt floor.

A hardy man is the cedar-whack—
    No part of the artful faker—
He clears the lands with his leather hands
    For sixty cents an acre.

The rain and snow and the blazin sun
    All lash at his hungry frame,
As he whacks away at the brush all day
    In Winter and Summer the same.

He wields his ax with the skillful wrists
    Of a sculptor carvin wood;
Now new grass frills on a thousand hills
    Where the cedar brake once stood.

He sorts and stacks the posts and staves,
　　Then hauls them to the yard
In his Model-T where he sells to me
　　For his beans and a can of lard.

Said The Hoot Owl to the Hen Hawk

Said the Hoot Owl to the Hen Hawk:
　　"Let's you and me agree
That you will work the day shift
　　And leave the night to me.

"The poultry of the barnyard
　　In the daytime range afar—
Which gives you easy pickin's
　　When I can't see where they are.

"But after dark it's different—
　　Then my stock takes a boost;
I quietly light among 'em
　　And pick one off the roost."

Said the Hen Hawk to the Hoot Owl:
　　"That deal suits me just swell;
We'll make an easy livin
　　While the chicken catches hell."

Bowie's Bones

Did you come to visit the Mission?
Well, stranger, I'll show you around;
They've got a museum in there in that room,
But they's more things outside they aint found.

You see that name on the gate there?
James Bowie wrote that while he's here—
He was tryin to locate the tribe's silver mine
And lived with 'em two or three year.

It's funny 'bout yarns gittin started
And after a feller or two
Have made up a windy and wrote in a book
We swaller it just like it's true.

F'r instance they claim Colonel Bowie
Was killed when the Alamo fell;
I never could figger how anyone knew—
Nobody was left there to tell.

James Bowie warn't killed in that battle—
It's a positive fact and I know.
I dug up his carcass back there in the hills,
And I got it right here for to show.

I was huntin them jack loads of silver
That Bowie was tryin to find;
I've searched for that treasure for forty-odd year—
They call it the Lost Bowie Mine.

Not far from this San Saba Mission
I was diggin an old Indian mound
And uncovered his knife and a couple of guns
And silver slugs scattered around.

His skeleton lay there beside 'em,
Where the Indians had put him away—
They caught him a-stealin their secret, you know,
And shot a hole through him one day.

Well, stranger, I'm proud that I met you;
Come around to my wagon sometime;
Them museum folks charge yuh two bits a look—
You can see Bowie's bones for a dime.

The King of the County Fair

A chestnut foal on tremblin legs
Is nudgin his mother's thigh,
While Old Trav lolls in the stable shade
And stares with a dreamy eye.

A half-smile plays on his wrinkled cheek
As he visions the golden flare
Of June Bug racin the Texas tracks—
The King of the County Fair.

With stockin legs and full-blazed face—
A meteor trimmed in white—
He left the post and he thundered home
Like a rocket in its flight.

He was not born of a purple line—
They say that his blood was cold.
They have not written his homely name
Where the blue-grass colts are sold.

He only raced at the county fairs,
Where the cheaper horses run;
But he loved to race, he was born to race,
And he ran like a champion.

His offspring ran with his blazin speed—
As all good horsemen knew;
So they bought his colts and changed their names—
Now they race where the grass is blue.

No horse may show at the major tracks
That carries a common stain,
So the stud book forges a royal line
For the colts of the June Bug strain.

But Old Trav knows, as he pets the foal
And smiles with a dreamy stare,
That the little mite of tan and white
Indeed is a royal heir.

And he knows the winners from coast to coast—
Because he is always there—
Are the sons and daughters of old June Bug,
The King of the County Fair.

The Substitute

    Oh, the honor and the glory
That the football heroes get
    Is well deserved—they battle hard;
They earn their cheers; and yet—
    Another on that ball club
I stand to give salute
    And pay him homage any day—
The lowly substitute.

    Now fate decrees that only boys
Of strong physique can play,
    And though the others practice long
And tough it out each day
    Through mud and sweat and bitter cold
To win the cherished call—
    They know their mates will represent
The Varsity this Fall.

    No praises sung at evening
When these weary lads pass by—
    The first-string are the cynosure
Of every maiden's eye.
    No tales to tell their kiddies
In the long, gray after days;
    We all forget in shouting—
It's the substitute who pays.

    No "letter" for his labors
When the long, hard season ends;

    He's always looking forward
When another year begins.
    If he wins or if he doesn't,
You will always hear me root
    For that bruised and disappointed kid,
The lowly substitute.

Duty

    If our home town needs improving,
As they all most surely do,
    Well, that's you and you and you and me—
We need improving, too.

    For a town's the folks that's in it,
And we write upon the scroll;
    And the record we have written
There reflects our very soul.

    So we owe a solemn duty
To our neighbors and our friends
    To do our home town honor
And to serve her noblest ends.

    It's a whole lot more important
Than vain glory or renown
    Just to be the kind of feller
Who does something for his town.

A Sermon

I've done a lot of thinkin
On the vanity and sin
   Of the things folks deem important
In this world we're livin in.

A lot of people spend their means
On empty show and sham—
   As if it really mattered
Or amounted to a damn.

They may profess the teachings
Of the lowly Nazarene,
   And make a lot of noble vows
That they don't really mean.

They need to learn that Heaven
Is always out of reach
   Of the folks who talk religion
But don't practice what they preach.

I sometimes doubt that schoolin
Is really worth the dough—
   When I see the sad condition
Of a lot of folks I know.

Why, what's the use of readin
Til your eyeballs bat and burn
   If you aint a-gonna practice
The few good things that you learn?

I'll take an old wood-hauler
Who can't even read or write
   To a constipated plutocrat
Who reads a book each night.

For his simple heart is humble
And he lives close to the sod—
   He labors in communion
With his neighbor and his God.

When the Books of Time are balanced
And we answer that last call—
   We may find the old wood-hauler
Is the richest one of all.

So a little real religion
Might help you and me a lot
   To polish up our mem'ry
On some things we've clear forgot:

That happiness is not for sale—
God's purpose starts and ends,
   And reaps its richest harvest
In the hearts of honest men.

Old Blue

I dreamt I was a kid again—
The world was bright and new;
  Beside me lay my target-gun
And my faithful houn—Old Blue.

  His ears were gnawed and floppy
And his ribs stuck through his hide;
  You could almost look plum through him
And inspect the other side.

  His eyes were kinda soulful—
Like a sinner knelt to pray;
  I don't know why, but God just made
And old houn dog that way.

  His mammy was a coon-dog,
And I raised him from a runt;
  So, he got his talents honest—
And that dog could really hunt.

  Did you ever climb the mountain
When the night was clear and cold;
  When the moon had worked her magic
Like Aladdin's Lamp of old;

  When the varmints were abundant
And their furs were rich and prime,
  With a bell-voiced, bayin coon-dog
Like Old Blue? That's life sublime!

To some folks Education
Is the Law of Text and Rule;
Some regard the Mill of Knowledge
As the Ivy-mantled School;

But the moral of the story,
In life's colored catalogue,
    May be learned out in the moonlight
From a flop-eared huntin dog.

Worldly honors shrink in stature
As the years mount one by one—
    And my journeys reminiscent
Take me back when I was young.

In the cloistered hall of mem'ry
Where the Old excels the New,
    There I warm my jaded spirit
By the embers—with Old Blue.

Values

Oh, the glamour and the clamor
That attend affairs of state
    Seem to fascinate the rabble
And impress some folks as "great."

But the truth about the matter
In the scale of loss and gain—
    Not one inauguration's worth
A good slow two-inch rain.

Blacksnake Bill

(Dedicated to Coke R. Stevenson)

When the shadows of the evenin softly stroll across the hills,
And the fever of the busy day is done;
   When the flamin fires of sunset quietly smolder into night,
And the stars report for duty, one by one;

   Then I turn in recollection to my happy childhood days,
And to one whose name in rapture holds me still:
     Ah, that noble old frontiersman, now a legend of
         the West—
That rawhide Texas freighter—Blacksnake Bill.

   From the Llano to San Saba he was known to one and all,
And his fame had spread beyond the Kickapoo—
     For regardless of the weather or the steepness of the hill,
Old Bill would always bring the wagon through.

   Now, he made our town on Tuesdays—about an
       hour by the sun—
He'd come in sight way down the windin lane;
     My perch upon the gatepost has become a hallowed spot
Where in memory he passes by again.

   I can see his loaded wagon pullin into Cherokee,
With a six-horse team a-tuggin in the sand;
     They were leanin in the collar 'cause Old Bill
        was talkin loud—
Like a King enthroned, he sat, in full command.

    He was loaded down with treasure—like a galleon
        with gold—
And I quickly ran to meet him on the hill;
    Then I climbed-up on the wagon, and proudly into town
I rode beside my hero—Blacksnake Bill.

    A goodly crowd had gathered, and Old Bill
        put on a show—
His blacksnake whip struck lightnin from the air;
    It sounded like the Civil War had done broke out again,
But on the team he never touched a hair.

He pulled-up on the vacant lot right next to Mitchell's Store,
Then scrambled down upon the doubletree—
   Yelled, "Howdy, Folks"—unhooked the team,
     and with a gentle hand
To the broad back of the wheel horse lifted me.

   Now, I've had my share of honors as the sands of life
     have run,
But if bound to single out my greatest thrill—
   I would have to choose the moment when I rode that
     wheel horse down
To water at the creek with Blacksnake Bill.

   Oh, he's long since gone to Glory, and his horses
     with him, too,
For the trains and trucks consigned them to the Fates—
   But he's freightin up in Heav'm, and he's puttin on a show
For the crowds that hang around the Pearly Gates.

   And of all the old compadres in the Halls of Paradise—
Where the reg'stered herd is cut out from the rest—
   In my book of top-performers who have gone
     to their Reward,
Old Blacksnake Bill, The Freighter, is the best.

The Big Convention

There are many wholesome pleasures
That delight the human soul—
    For simple beauties in this world abound;
But the sweetest entertainment
    Is the all-day singin bee—
Where old friends meet, for dinner on the ground.

I remember how we gathered
At the arbor on the creek—
    Where they held the big Convention every Spring.
And the folks from counties far and near
    All laid their burdens down—
And joyously they made the hillsides ring.

There they met in sweet communion
As they voiced their prayers in song—
    Humbly grateful for the blessings of the Lord;
Then they all adjourned for dinner—
    And the miracle to me
Was the bounties that the Smoke House did afford.

I never saw the like of food
The women folks prepared—
    And us kids just stared and squirmed upon a log
Until Old Brother Thompson
    Had returned our reverent thanks—
Then we filled up like a hungry huntin dog.

Now they claim before a singin
Folks ought not to eat a-tall—
　　That it interferes with how to hold your breath;
But I knew some old "tune-histers"
　　Who could founder and still sing,
Until they starved Caruso plum to death.

　　I remember well the mixed quartette,
The feature of the show—
　　Each member was an artist all his own.
And of all my youth's ambitions,
　　The dream to sing a part
In that comp'ny was the greatest I have known.

　　Aunt Nina was an alto
Who was wonderful to hear,
　　While Miss Betty's soft soprano was sublime!
And the bass of Old Man Tobin
　　Seemed to come out of a well,
While Pa's tenor took it two rows at a time.

　　Then that chorus, so compelling,
Seemed to waft our hearts on high,
　　And the light of Heaven shone so bright and fair
As the congregation shouted
　　And each soul proclaimed the hope,
"When the Roll Is Called Up Yonder I'll Be There."

    Oh, I know they're still a-singin
    Over on the other shore—
        And when Gabriel blows his trumpet by and by,
    We will join with the angels
        Singin Glory to the Lord—
    And hold a Big Convention in the Sky.

Service

If the road is rough and rocky as this life we journey through,
Then we ought to take a little time to move a rock or two.
For there is no greater pleasure that the passing years can send
Than the deep-down satisfaction when you've helped along a friend.

I Built My House upon a Hill

        I built my house upon a hill
            That I might search horizons far
        To find my vagrant spirit lost
            Upon some dim, unchristened star.

        I built my house upon a hill
            Where clouds caress my tousled hair.
        I think perhaps that God and I
            Can get acquainted better there.

Ambition

I'm a plain one-mule share-cropper
From way down on Gander Slough,
   Where I've been a-dry-land farmin with my Paw;
But it go so hot this Summer
   I just dried-up on the cob—
And that decided me to study law.

Oh, a noble trait—Ambition—
And the thirst for legal lore
   Is an attribute of which great men are made;
But the strongest inspiration
   To high education's march
Is a balky mule at a hundred in the shade.

Yes—there's somethin most appealin
When you're thirsty, hot and tired,
   And you've tromped them middles till your feet are raw,
'Bout an air-conditioned office
   With your name plate on the door—
And the magic title—Counsellor-At-Law.

So I think I'll go to college—
Where they do their work indoors—
   And cram a little learnin in my craw;
Then I'll open-up an office
   On Congress Avenue
And practice me a little City Law.

The Sheriff's Widow

I can see her by the window
When the evening sun is low—
   Just a shadow in the twilight
Rocking slowly to and fro.

   She's the widow of the sheriff,
And her hair is silver gray—
   And I reckon I was one of those
Who made it turn that way.

   They were living in the jail house
At the time I boarded there—
   And she never failed to feed me
Or to mention me in prayer.

   The sheriff was an honest man,
And "right" was all he knew—
   And when he started on a job
He always saw it through.

   He was firm, but he was humble.
Course he never saved a dime,
   'Cause the county didn't pay him
Half enough for half his time.

   Still he served them long and faithful,
Fair alike to friend and foe—
   Stood his ground for law enforcement—
Yet the people let him go.

Now his widow sits and ponders
On the days when they were young—
How their hearts with pride were swollen
When his star on him she hung.

And she's happy in the knowledge
That he served with his last breath
The State he loved so truly—
While she slowly starves to death.

The Old Nightwatchman

He was standin on the corner
With his two guns hangin low,
   Tellin how he killed a bandit
On the border long ago.

   His old boots had made the winter
And his big hat maybe ten,
   But the night-law's hat in Llano
Takes a right smart breakin in.

   It needs a bullet hole or two
To make the crease set right,
   And all soaked-up with sweat and blood,
And the dirt of a tough gang fight.

   Sure he sounded kinda windy,
Til you got to know him good;
   Like a lot of folks, peculiar,
And most times misunderstood.

   His whole life was law-enforcement,
And he always looked the part,
   And the tales he told of exploits bold
Were the dreams of a hungry heart,

   As he trudged his lonely, shadowed beat
Through the storms of soul that blow;
   Each long dark mile each long black night
Through the dust and rain and snow.

He knew each petty thief and thug,
And the "cons" who'd knock a knob;
He wore his badge where all could see,
For he loved his night-watch job.

Now they say a stray shot got him,
As he made his nightly round;
And he died there in the harness
By his pistol on the ground.

You may sing hymns to the faithful,
And high anthems to the brave;
I'll drop a tear and plant a rose
On the old nightwatchman's grave.

Hard Times

It's hard times down in Texas shore nuf;
I mean that things are really gettin rough;
I've quit my tom cat prowlin
Since I took the weddin vow;
I've traded my old pickup
For an old two-gallon cow;
The gals who hustled honky tonks
All take in washin now,
For it's hard times down in Texas, shore nuf.

Pete Wood'ard

Pete Wood'ard was the scavenger
In our town, years ago—
  Before we built the sewer
And the place began to grow.

A most respected citizen—
And necessary to—
  He did the job that other folks
Just plain refused to do.

He drove the privy-wagon
When the outhouse was in flower—
  And his labors lent effulgence
To that aromatic bower,

Where the soul, in deep reflection,
Often dreamed the hours away—
  And a sense of sweet contentment
Filled complete the summer day.

He was punctual and proper;
And his work no critic knew,
    For he gave that extra service—
Whether just one hole or two.

    No, he shirked not aught of duty—
Whether cleaning one or ten—
    By the lime that he had scattered
You could tell where Pete had been.

    I can hear him now a-whistlin
Like a harbinger to tell
    That he soon would be at our house—
And we'd have to wait a spell.

    So, I salute Pete Wood'ard,
A servant and a friend,
    Patrolman of the Privy—
He was faithful to the end.

Your Eyes Are Brown

Your eyes are brown; my eyes are blue.
    But you see me, and I see you.

So what care we for shade or color
    As long as we can see each other?

Nylon Avenue

There is a town not far from here
I often travel through,
   Quite famous for a boulevard
Called Nylon Avenue.

'Tis very wide and lined along
With mansions richly done;
   And from a proud and stately hill
Looks down on Rabbit Run.

In wonderment I gaze upon
Those massive marble walls
   And vaulted domes which tower above
Their gilded banquet halls—

And ponder that a friend of mind,
Who Fortune's smile has won,
   Has lately moved upon the hill
From down on Rabbit Run.

But now a strained and fretful air
Pervades his erstwhile joy,
   And things once viewed with unconcern
Now worry and annoy.

Now barren, frustrate and forlorn
The hopes my friend once knew—
   When young ambition fired his climb
Up Nylon Avenue.

The old town clock in the Courthouse tower,
He knows the spell of the midnight hour:
　　The moonlight dancing upon the street—
The watchman pacing his lonely beat—
　　A rooster crowing of battle scars—
A houn dog baying the distant stars—
　　The whimpering owl by the old millrace—
A boy and a girl in love's embrace—
　　A good night kiss and a word of prayer,
By the old town clock on the Courthouse square.

The Ticket

If to frailties of mortals as a critic I'm unkind,
I'm afraid that old Saint Peter to my virtues may be blind.
But if I love my neighbor and upon my brother wait,
I kinda think that ticket will pass me through the gate.

Human Nature

You can study human nature from Creation up to now;
You can analyze and speculate on why and when and how;
But you'll find no truer proverb than that often wailed
　　complaint,
"They're fer you when you're winnin; they're agin you
　　when you aint."

Bonnie Bird
(1890–1917)

(Dedicated to Doe Bowman)

I've handled lots of hosses
That could run a little bit,
   And all my life I've watched 'em—fast and slow;
But old Bonnie Bird by Rondo—
   Take it all the way around—
Was the Queen of Quarter Hosses for my dough.

We would match 'er when she's ready;
We would start 'er when she weren't—
   But old Bonnie Bird, she never failed to fire.
And a-prancin or a-limpin,
   Or too heavy with a foal—
She was mighty apt to beat 'em to the wire.

I recall that day in Roswell
When the "money" liked the Bay—
   'Cause they figgered that old Bonnie Bird was through;
But she cocked that little twisted ear
   And shook her stubby tail
And settled with the boys in "22."

Yep, she beat some purty good uns
For a quarter of a mile,
   And she'd give a little daylight now and then;
She didn't mind it muddy,
   And she didn't mind it hot—
All Bonnie cared to know was "where and when."

Now there's been some faster hosses,
So the record books declare—
    And I won't flat-footed say it just aint so;
But the day they clocked them ponies
    Old Bonnie wasn't there—
So me and her just say, "We wouldn't know."

I'll be out at Ruidoso's
All-American this fall—
    It's Labor Day, and all the chips are blue;
I'll be settin there a-dreamin
    As they thunder down the stretch—
And watch old Bonnie win in "22."

Abe Galloway

(A DIRGE)

Now bleak winter blankets autumn
As Life's curtain last descends;
And the pain of final parting
From these hills in anguish rends

Cherished ties of love and laughter
Abe and I from boyhood knew;
Riding range and trail together
Under darkened skies and blue.

Heaven writes the rules for nature:
Golden leaves to chilling blasts
Yield reluctantly their season,
Then, like Abe, they fall at last.

He will find no fear in shadows,
Where most mortals trembling tread;
He will boldly ride in darkness
Through the hills where we were bred.

And though I by night am daunted
He will lead me as we go,
Cause old Abe's not scared of darkness,
He was black himself you know.

Cactus Jack

    I've knowed a lot of fellers
Who talked mighty well informed.
    They'd expound on any subject
Once they got their motor warmed.

    But no man of my acquaintance,
When you cull the entire pack,
    Could figure human nature,
Like my old friend, Cactus Jack.

    He was quiet in conversation,
Never had too much to say;
    He used the scales of logic
In a horse-sense sort of way.

    He kinda had a feeling
For the quirks of mortal man;
    He could always spot a phony
As not many people can.

    Fuss'n Feathers didn't faze 'im,
Nor big-shots in striped pants,
    If it wasn't twenty carat
He could tell it at a glance.

    They say he went to Washington
To hold some office there;
    Don't know what-all he learnt them boys
Cept three's will beat two pair,

And that workin for a livin
And the Lord's what makes a man;
   Our Freedom is our gospel,
Not some socialistic plan.

Old Jack'll soon be ninety,
And I wish him ninety more;
   He's taught some lessons we should learn
And, I mean, learn for shore.

It seems to this old cowhand,
At the very least excuse,
   Things we usta hold as sacred
We now handle awful loose.

We had better pay attention
To what Cactus has to say,
   If we aim to keep our country
And not give it plum away.